THE DAYS
OF
ME AND GOD

a poetic autobiography

by BILLYE OKERA

The Days of Me and God

Graphic Design: Torri Thoto

ISBN: 1-938373-09-X
ISBN 13: 978-1-938373-09-1
Printed in the United States

© **BW** *Broad Wing Press ©2016, 2019*
Lanham, Maryland

DEDICATION

FOR J, D and A

TABLE OF CONTENTS

PROLOGUE

DAYBREAK LIGHTNESS

This is not the dark night of my soul
This is not a day of lament or torment
Or kneeling at the mourners' bench
Moanin' and groanin' for deliverance
And repentance and self-flagellations for sin
That God Himself don't remember nothin' about.

This is not a time of sorrow and worry
For tomorrow's not given me
Or torrid memories out of the sea
Of many witnesses gone before
Who bore me over and some about
Without a shout at kindness or blessing
Or even confessing
The wrongs they heaped upon the head of innocence.

This is not a dirge dance –
    Symphony in C-sharp minor
Mournin' over what was lost
Or what it cost me to let go of you
Or them, or things, or places, or systems,
Or rituals, and residual recklessness,
Or failed relationships that just failed:
No makeup test required.

I tell this tale for one long mired in melancholy
Long limping on broken promises
Long lifting other's men's burdens
Long helping and healing and heralding
And reaching and teaching and reaching out
And giving out of an account long over drawn
And due upon receipt.

This is not the dark night, truth be told,
But my daybreak song. A bursting through to Christ,
Not just of hope
    In something pulled from stagnant air
As public prayer, or purloined prophecy
And practiced praise.
This is the song I raise:
Mighty days about
As I dance and shout about this sanctuary
No longer weary or forlorn
I have borne the cross left for me to carry
Learned the lessons listed in His Word
Heard the hearty welcomes of the bridegroom
Into His house with not one wretched word
    For growing old
But just his daybreak lightness in my soul.

INKLING

So you know that you know
That you know, that you know
That you don't know.
But you do hope
Because love hopes all things!

WE ARE FOUR

We are four my sisters and I
The younger
    Born in the mournful bow of a treble cleft
Blended and consumed in constricted reverie
She lowers her brow in humble manipulations
Graces her days giving God glory.
Her story
    Not yet revealed concealed in unspoken woe
She, my grandfather's favorite
My grandmother's pride
Eyed in the eye of Pentecostal preference. . .
The chosen one.

She is the crown's frown – my second self
Eyes grasp eyes daring affirmation of secrets held
In and of herself she towers
    Low in the tall of inclement anger
She can't unearth her dead.
Even with the earth smoothed down
Her ghost only play upon her midnights,
Saying nothing of losing her
And letting her go.

My first – the bridge naming the pictures
Held in my body
She is memory of my father's face
A place, a mirrored cabinet
A patch of my mother's hair lain within
The sin of my father held in my grandmother's hand.
She the gluing of imagery and reality
Weeping in her body the salty tears
Of a pre-verbal child.

And I – I am all of them
The veil held between –
Now shuttered asunder
Inhaling the thunder of the musty air.
I was there to greet them
At the opening of the womb
The tomb of our coming cinched
In the fist of a man who could not love
And a woman who knew no better
Than to love him.

Soon we will come to the valley of our parting
Soon the flexing of goodbyes
The simple cries of my mother on her deathbed
"Take care of each other"
Smothered in the tales we had to tell
Closeted in the anger of secrets
And spirit guides
Unable to love or save.
Well, neither cradle or grave
Has robbed the bond between
Nor the mean years sense
For which we seek concord.

REMEMBER THE OLD DAYS

A poem of remembrance of when we called on the name of Jesus.

Remember the old days
Remember the old ways of our fathers,
    Our mothers
Wednesday noon-time prayer meeting
Running to Mother's house from school
Calling Mother Crawley from next door
Remember the prophecy come forth
What she expected of us
Never spoken, but intuited
"Women of God you will be
Singers of song you will be
And He will be lifted up".

Remember the time of our youth
Remember the truth of the Gospel
Mashed down and pressed together blessing
Tavy's grands in the choir stand
In the Sunday school
Ruled by all she knew
And all she knew was Jesus.
Remember the cloth upon the brow
At tarrying service
Tongues aflame from youthful lips
The gift of the Spirit
On the heads of babes
And He will be lifted up.

Remember the days gone by
Our cries, and why, and whys
Of no answer but the mystery of faith.
Remember that grace, amazing
Flowing in the heat of warfare
The enemy confounded and astounded
By the power of God.
Remember we are overcomers
Readying for that overcoming to the promised-land
Remembering - '
He Who Sits Upon the throne' of heaven
     In victory and Glory
And He will be lifted up!

SHADOW SORROW

The shadow sorrow that my heart acquired
In ancient rooms where-in my people prayed
And prophesied believing me inspired
Enough to catapult me from the grave.
But what I come to know was always phantom
Some nesting fear they held within their breast
Yet hid it tight in song and saintly anthem
While shedding ash and sack-cloth from their chest.
What word could they have given me for hoping?
What song to soothe the crying child bereft?
What strong elixir brewed for me for groping
An answer more explicative than death?
But oh, their feet would break down in a dance
As if there were some inkling of a chance.

NOTHING WAS HOLY THEN

Nothing was holy then!
Now looking back
It was all such a crime
Such a time of sorrow
And not knowing I called it holy
But holiness was so unholy
And the whole of the story is
That holiness won't be fooled.
Oh, for a time you think
Or for a wink in the midst of tragedy
But, putting old wine in new bottles
And sewing old fabric on new wool
And calling hate love
And violation salvation is travesty.
See, if it were left up to me
I would go back
And wreak havoc
On the heads of culpability
I would call them out
From their small places
Pray the hatred from their faces
And their hearts.
But, starting over from here
Trying to do it all again the right way
Having the right say, you know
STOP!
You beast. . .
STOP!
And let my child's heart alone
Has grown and old a weary dream
And a hollow scream
For days that will not come again.

REHOBOTH

When I was a child
God did things his way.
Beauty wrapped in trees
Birds, rain and bubbly lights at Christmas
Then hangin' high His own –
    Oak soaked in blood and pain
Love and death drawn alike from one source
Speaking absolute ambivalence.
I tried to understand what love that was.
I tried to understand
And pat my hands
And stomp my feet
At tarrying service on Sundays at 5pm.

But, I knew God shoulda' got it right the first time
Eden, apples, people and serpents together
    In he said,
        She said, it said
Sure for disaster.
And I thought, in creating all evil was expendable
And there was little need of menstrual cramps,
Lying lovers and stones peltin' prostitutes –
    And death.
But I figured I could call and all would be well
    When I was a child.

When I was a child I was always afraid.
Looking at cloud formations
Watchin' the sky for cracks
List'nin' for strong sounding trumpets from the east -
Contemplating fire.
I tried not being a liar –
    Takin' Madelyn's eraser in first grade
And Daddy's Gulden's mustard
And little Henry rubbing my leg under the table
Was by no means consensual.
But, God was always angry
And nothing I could do
Ever drew me close to Him certainly
    When I was a child.

When I was a child I'd hold myself in the night
Wishing someone were holding me
And that it was not rape -
God showing slight preference for rapist,
    Of course.
'Cause, I was rape-able, you understand -
Fat, nappy headed, virginal
And evidently needing violation,
I didn't scream or resist.
And when my mama walked into the house
I sealed my sin in stone
Washed blood and flushed it in a commode
And climbed beneath the covers. . . shivering.
Then - I suppose - he made love to her - go figure.
    When I was a child.

When I was a child Ed Sullivan was fine for Pearl Bailey
        And Nat Cole
But no soul motioned me to move from clips of the Holocaust
And bodies layin' rottin' piled in pits
And smoke seeping from crematoriums.
And, being small
And God being big - And mean - And responsible And awful
And full of love – suffering little children to come,
I came. And the places of my heart slammed silent.

Days floating on crystal air I am still there
Hiding behind chairs curling in corners
Head under tent from couch to couch
Held by fastenings of teddy bears
        And books strewn about.
You learn to shut things out:
Your grandfather beating your uncle – naked
 Somebody shaving your doll's head
And saying it was you
You standing in stairwells dress torn and hair undone
And Cousin Jerome wrestling himself on top of you
With them all watching,
With them ALL watching,
And not a one. . . coming to rescue.
        When I was a child.

When I was a child - those days –
        I didn't have a feeling God loved
Only waited for appropriate time and sin
So he could win
And do his God thing casting me away.
And I suppose,

Shoutin' in the aisles at Rehoboth was ok
Till Mother Dickerson led you to the air and the stare
Of folk outside on the corner on 8th and L
And all your feeling of doom came back - cold.
Now, being somewhat old
I remember that in my tent
I could forget Vampire Bats at Monroe School
And Elder Michaux's devil - at least for a while -
    When I was child.

I REMEMBER THE OLD DAYS

I remember the old days down on my knees
Pleasin' pastah and presbytery
Tarryin' for the Holy Ghost
Spoken syllable to rise from your gut
But for the demons standing by
And my cry in the arms of Motha D. . .
See...I am a saved girl, too
See...I am a good girl, too.
You shoulda' seen the sweat and the tears
And eight year-old fears
Floating through kick-ball games
And forbidden bird-land dance
Standing on my uncles shoe-straps
Tappin' to the sounds my Grand' condemned
As she hymned Wednesday noon-day prayer.
Prayer and praise and proper perfect girls
Lost in a whirl of secrets even God refused to see.

I remember the shout of organ run
        That pump of feeling
Beating down demons.
But for those of us who would not dance
A grim romance in darkness
Darkness dark as unbelief
Incredulous that others never raised a brow
To question how, or why or when
Sin and shame became the theme of life and breath.

I remember Cleveland and Mattie Moss
And tossing my nappy head from side to side
Hoping it would swing in the breeze
So someone would be pleased to throw a lap-rag
    About me
And see that the tears I cried
Weren't because I was breaking through to Christ
But breaking apart
For the vice and silence
Of those charged to love me.

I remember Black and White
And night-time Gospel music
And young-old people singing to ring in the Spirit
To bring Word to life with hand clap and tambourine
And the careening voices of the chosen few.
Chosen not by the lot of the hand of God
But the odd capricious circumstance
    Of beauty.

I remember the mothers of the church
Slaving in August-hot kitchens
Chicken-Chit'lin' dinners
And money for the building funds
And the pastor's aid and comfort.
Servin', slavin' and praisin' –
    Serving the 'mand' of God
So that God would nod
In agreement.

I remember the awesome Blackness of Tave
Waving her long black hair
As she walked the aisles of Rehoboth
In her first-lady hat
While the deacons spat tobacco on the Church lot.
There is a lot you could say about 8th and L
Winos, women, spirit and flesh
Circling the citadel of the saved
Braving anything but the truth.
Truth be told
Old, old pain
Remained behind those Greek-Orthodox walls
In the halls where pretty girls – light and fair
Caught the eye, while winking at the sight
Of the ones un-noticed.

 I remember when granny Irene died,
And we, the four of us, my sister and I
Cried in the aisles – alone -
There in the sanctuary of Rehoboth.
And the sages said, "Laugh when they die,
And Cry when they are born,"
And then hurried to send us home
 On a DC Transit bus.

'deed I remember the day Daddy was baptized
And how surprised we all were
When mother was baptized (again) with him
Happy she had caught her prey
Happy she had prayed on through
Though I still rue the sight
Of his violent beatings.

I remember they told her to tie her breast down
 So they would not move when she shouted -
And she did.
They told her not to wear her long black hair down The slope
        Of her back -
And she didn't.
They told her
To get a hat to cover her head in sanctuary
To pay in ten-percent
To pay in offering
To pay in feeding the bishop
To pay in working the altar –
And there would be a star
    In her crown.
And when it came, they only said –
The stroke in her brain was the devil
Her deeds not enough, no
Never, never, never enough!

He spoke in eloquence
Peppering' the threat of hell
With a "well Jesus"
And they all said "amen"
And sang what a friend Jesus was and is
Dismissing the fears of the broken child.

Acting as if (sometimes, but not much)
Even I would step into the aisle
Holding to a bench with one hand
Circling the air with the other
My hair sweated out
Spit slipping from my mouth

Worked-UP!
(Bishop Larr was far – far more
    The 'anointed' preacher than Elder Tuft)
And it was tough deciding to sit still
And swallow the pill of being the outsider
Never really feelin' that joining it.

I remember stepping outside of myself
 Watching - waiting (never praying)
Never, knowing to say "Jesus save me"
Not from sin, but for having to fight and thrive
In an atmosphere of apathy.
I remember waiting, watching, hoping
Someone knew enough to grab me by the hand
 And have me stand in my childhood as a child
And not confront God and man
As only grown-folk can.

 I remember the day the demons came,
    And the girl,
Curled in the corner, speaking gruff incantations
Spewing green spit
As they shewed
The mothers and babies from the room.
I remember thinking then
Green spit
Gruff words
My demons were those heard
In my grandfather yelling his curses
That no verse nor psalm obliterated – "you dummy,"
"You dummy," then hand me a nickel
To fetch his Red-Line News from Larry's store
On the corner of Newton Street.

Children see God in their father's face
In the grace of their mother's folded arms at table.
No one thought God's love is human touch
God's light in the shinning eyes
Of those who don't despise themselves.
I remember always as a child
God always ask something of me
That was absent in me.
Others had it: they quaked with electric pulses
Their bodies jerked about,
Their feet shouting step by step, side by side
 Choreographed dance and show
Showing God they knew how
       To worship.

God, I wish I could remember, "Jesus loves me"
And having sang it
Had it permeate
And stake a claim on my child-mind.

What was it of God they missed?
That I missed – and that begs me now
In ritual
     In rigid righteousness
          In Easter dresses
               In pressed hair and painted nails
Never healing the hurt
Hungering for a heart-song of redemption.

Long – long before my coming of age
Long – long before I knew
God doesn't show up
Only at top-ten tabernacles,

24

For there were places in me
Only Spirit could descend
To win my sanity.
Only Christ could light the fire
To purge toxic faith and replace it
With his love.
Not standing on show
Not standing on circumstance
Not hampered by memory
Not dependent on crowd noise
Or the need for the voices of the boys of my youth
    At Rehoboth
Singing "The Blood That Jesus Shed for Me"
Because now I am free to sing it for myself
And Christ knows I am free
    I am free!
        Indeed!

NIGHT COMETH

For the night cometh
And all the holocaust present scenes
Of death and damnation:
Little Black girl sitting second-row center
Grandma's hat shadowing the pew
You know it is you, the sinner
Bursting hell wide open
Teeth of the damned piercing your side.
There is no hide-and-seek refuge
For the seeker of all knows all
Sees all and all is about you:
Little child born in sin you know you could not know
Born into history not your making
Born braving the pitiable pool
Of people placing blame.

For the night cometh
You know it is you who sees
Spit stains and sewage
Smearing your grandma's Persian.
Mixing the smells of Chicken-Chitlin' thanks
With pranks of man and boy devastating
Erasing the childhood dreams
Defacing childhood memory
And your screams in the night silent.

For the night cometh
No child can labor there
Where touch a demon
And dried tears

Stain lids lowered to the sound
Of bishop blowing brimstone and ash
As the sash of the crinoline
Lay on the floor behind the door
 Of the mangled-child.

BY THAT PLOT OF SOIL REFLECTING

By that plot of soil reflecting
As the blue of sky projecting

Images of deep dark chambers
Images of rock and ridges

Going lower there's a sinking
Lower, lower there's a sinking

Stripping all that touch surrendered
Dust and clay no coy pretender

Have we not performed our dances
Did we not sing "Rock of Ages"

"Rock of Ages" in the choirs
Dance of dances to the lyre

Did we not consume the pages
Pray and prostrate to the sages

Why this silence in the narthex
What these whispers weeping silence

From the ridges of the mountain
Can't they blow a kiss from heaven

Show me, show me spirits walking
Hear me, hear me spirits talking

When the last of time is over
And they cover me with clover

Kindly lower me to heaven
Kindly take this cup unproven

Can't we reckon with you hangman
Bribe you hangman with our mammon

Is there not just one objection
Can we not appeal this verdict

By that plot of soil reflecting
You accepting, You rejecting

As the blue of sky projecting
As the doves fly upward truly

Will I soar and ever be?

UP HERE IN THIS ROOM

I am up here in this room, Jesus
They telling me to do it this way
And dem others saying do it dat way
I ain't got no clue to who You are
Except some star
    Rode the sky like two thousand years ago
And the show was on. . .
PBS and CNN.
And every sin I repented for since
Don't make no sense to me
Cause you see. . . I'm always on the end of it
Hurting and trying to find reason
Tryin' to feel
    Tryin' to heal
        Tryin'. . .
To discern commandment from bull-crap
Cause it never sat well wid me
Dat every time I see collar and Cross
Something be lost,
Something carted outta me
And nothing been left inside.

I been tryin' to hide this rage
I been tryin' to stage real forgiveness
And kindness
And solidarity
And really somewhere beneath this trial
There is a load of guilt and recrimination
And sorrow old as the nations of Israel
    And Islam
        And dark
As the head of my mother wrapped in Kinte.

I'm up here in this room, Jesus
Wid people telling me hands off
Walk straight,
Gate to hell as wide
As the legs you opened for last night's lover.
Never cover the truth I say
'Cause it's only under cover I gets to forget
This split between my soul and me
And I be freer than a bird rising.

Baptize me in shadow
Circumcise this lack
Take me back, if you can, and if you will,
To the place where, spilled upon a tree,
You saw me
Then as now. . . a child. . .
Hiding in the third row balcony
When Bishop Carr fainted and the church
Went up in frenzy
And I sweated my hair out
So's you couldn't get a comb through it
Cause I thought, to do it, You would love me.

But it was still Maize
And the pretty girls with curls
With the fellas waving fans about them
And they hemmed and hawed
    And I was awed how soul
Could leave body to never return
And you could yearn for it and yearn for it
But, IT was written,
And there was no petition for reconsideration.

31

So, I'm here in this room, Jesus
Down de stairs
Way behind de laundry
Wid de dirt under de rugs
Cause dis stuff be hidden away.
But, I have swept de floor a bit
And the cousins will come tomorrow
And we will play Monopoly
Or Bid-Whiz
And not one would have kissed the face
Of the woman of sorrow.
And no one would have asked after her sanity
They'll just assume the bloom on the rose
Was absent thorn
And her mourning pliable as cotton.

Come home, my sistah.
To yourself - come home
And let those of meager spirit
Stay in the amen corner
While you walk among beggar and thief
And find relief with your head
        Held gracefully upward.

Come home, my sistah. You forgot your place
Was a place of total emptying,
And what will come will come
As what was owed
Even, should it be not what was asked
You will still bask in the knowing that you tried
And never lied about disgust
      And death
          And darkness.

Speak to these waters about you
And don't drown!
For down in the valley
Dry bones arise
      And survive
Dancing towards tomorrows!

IN THAT SIMPLE ROOM
ON THOSE SIMPLE WEDNESDAYS

In that simple room
On those simple Wednesdays
Something of fear
Something of fasting
Something craving fast get-aways
Restrained. Made to stay
Made to bray
In my grandma's parlor
Something of faith kindled by gramma's spirit
Something of her rotund breast and her chest
Heaving heavy hands to the sky
Being pulled down
Being handed down
Being forced down
Being hammered down
Driven down inside not to be questioned
Something so sure, surety
    Was sullied.
Faith fractured in the face
Rigidity rapped on hands
Horror hidden in hearts
A silencing eye and a grimace
a "not in here chile
    Not in this House of Zion
        Not in the House of God."

In that simple room
On those simple Wednesdays
Something coming out from them
Something seeking exit from them
    Into you
Not much of love
But of fear
Fear and anguish over death
Petitions for reconsideration denied
Angst and pain and fear and supplication
Folded hands, knees bent, weeping. . .
Weeping, tarrying, praying, biting at the bit,
Coughing up spit
Stomping on the heads of demons
Thrashing and crashing on the floor –
    Hoping.

Hoping somebody would come with another witness
Another story to tell
Another praise to offer
Another moment in another time in another universe
    Not here
Not of being nine and only thinking to escape death
Death and wrath, fire, lightnings and thunderings
Down from the smoky mountain
Hoping God would see your hand first
Hoping He would choose you
And that you would have the right answers
Instead of these questions
These bangings in your head.
This terror in your gut
Never praise, but dread
    Raised to the third heaven.

Eppie on the sun porch on Park Place
Speaking in tongues
Holy Ghost on this chile…
Holy Ghost gon' ta use this chile…
Motha Douglas grand gone stand fo' God anointed
Appointed by prophecy
    And the holy see of hands laid.
Hoping they would not touch me
Hoping they would not speak of me
Hoping they would not speak to me
And see the tears
And the fears
And the falling out
And the shame of lap rags placed
On nine year old knees
So no one sees premature glory.

Mother Crawley
Dark, dark woman of God
Blackened skin shining of Vaseline
And tough hands cleaning white folk's houses
White dress covering all possibility of passion
Head rag denying all possibility of glory
She alone responsible to get this
Ju-ju jerkin', rockin' and talkin' to God
Having Him nod or speak in a noticeable voice
So she could tell the other and the other run with it
Give it out as word from Sinai
Defying others to charge it
    Change it or rename it.

Bishop stepping in a minute and then out
Before the cock crows
Out of site and out of mindfulness
Blessing the children of the blessed
Mother Douglas and her grands
Raising them up in the admonition
Raising them up in the tradition
Tall tales and tight lips
Can't sip the cup of this truth.

Mama would not know Wednesdays
Mama would not show Wednesdays
Noontime prayer too much
Noontime tears interfering
With smoke and gin
And men folk waiting for the spoils
Of my father's dementia and death.

Motha Dear and Frankie:
Cranky old woman Motha Dear
Passed from place to place when Frankie died
Cried in that simple room
On those simple Wednesday' noondays
For Elder Tuft to call her bluff
And puff on what was left of her private places
    Rusted shut.
Submitting in that simple room
On those simple Wednesdays
Noondays and Mother Crawley
Noondays and the Bishop's wife
Noondays and my grandma Tave
Holding us late to lunch

Late for school a block away
Praying without ceasing
Praying before eating
Praying for obedience
Praying
Praying
Praying
Praying
In that hot-noon parlor
Paisley priestesses being born again
And again and again – My sisters and I –
Praying and testifying
Telling of our visitations
Of visions and dreams
But for the *one* disappearing deep
  Into her darkness. . .
   Silent.

WHY I STAYED HOME ASH WEDNESDAY

Why I stayed home Ash Wednesday
Asked God about it
Seeking significance on net-long pages
Praising Catholic holy days not mentioning Pentecostals
Though no longer Pentecostal
It felt so Pentecostal trying not to posit some things
Like why I stayed home Ash Wednesday
Thinking I'd found some answers, losing them
Searching ever again – growing old
Remembering man is dust
Growing old
In circuitous rituals ravaging time
Wanting for rhyme or reason.

The ashes, the ashes, the ashes, I say
The ashes, the ashes, the ashes
Like the labyrinth I challenged before my fall
Waiting for twist or turn to prove Son-worthy
Or demons to rise from the mazed ground
Disguised as a god dressed in druid linen.

There must be sacrifices I am told
Penitence and prophesyings,
Flagellations and fastings,
Forty days and nights of icy certainties –
That I vex God about everyday anyway
Inquiring what more they might want of me
What more does He want? Though bowed low
Waiting the lightning strike.

Just this week
I have paid tithe and offering
Cleaned the parlor adjacent the sanctuary
Sang in the Choir
Fed the homeless at the shelter
And thought. Thought. THIUGHT long, long hours
Of roof repairs, Bible-bowl
And the ruddy, ruddy goo spewing itself
    Into the narthex.

Just this week
I have thought, Thought, THOUGHT
Thought of nothing but God
And God, and God, and God, and God
Asking Him if I, alone, am crazy
Or does the world speak to Him
On an hourly basis too.
    Nonstop
Continuous dialogue of the grave
And why my mother couldn't have stayed
    A few moments longer,
Deeding what she knew of grace.

I have forty days to figure this out
Forty days to wait this out
Looking for Lenten wonder and shekinah glory
To overtake these fears of "mistaken roads
Ending in mistakes."

Last Sunday, there was communion
    As the Sunday before
        As the Sunday before
As the Sunday before – me in perpetuity
Reckoning communion consummates redemption –
Every Sunday after short, short services,
Shorter than the three-hour prophecies
 Bishop Carr preached
In Apostolic/Pentecostal rantings
Saying search yourself, repent
    Or die.
Shorter than years of fear festering in children
Bullied to baptismal pools.

I stayed home because I was tired
Pain piping down my arms
Like a beginning heart attack that wouldn't come
That I wished would come somehow
Something to shake me loose
And cause some reaction other than
Deep
    Dull
        Dogma.

I stayed home because I was weary;
The grandkids wore me out, yet I love the grandkids–
They are closer to God, and I've needed no prodding
Laughing with them, and wiping tears.
No one has wiped mine dry,
And I could not imagine myself
Coming to an empty room
With black ashen cross upon my head
And my heart like the dead
    In a tomb.

THE BOYS IN THE QUARTET SINGING

We speak little or nothin' of Nathan
 Or how the clamminess of Cyanide and Kool-aide
Travelled past the covens of Jonestown
And reached the choir-stand at Rehoboth.
Carl and Monroe and Isaac and Ronald
The boys in quartet singing,
"The Blood that Jesus Shed". . .
Was no potion to wake the dead
    Lying in frozen stupor
Thinking God came to lonely souls desperate
For joining. . . following even a fool.
In my dream Sister Berry played
And Sharon sang a jazzy rendition of "Just as I am."
Nothing was "just"
A lot a primping
And curling and pressing went into it
And Flo, sensing the competition
    Sizzled playful side-cracks
        Of venom.
In my dream – I was the choir leader
Picking the songs – all of them wrong
Too short and absent harmony
I was in the wrong place – again.

FEEL SOMETHIN'

Feel somethin'!
Even the bad days feel them
Soiled and full of shit-things happenin'
Hands pushed away. Feel the fear
Passing of another year – month – day - hour –
　　Not knowing
Whose bed will satisfy
Not caring anyway. Any old body will do
Strickin' and worn and well up the way. At least
Pull from that nothin'
Somethin' to offer your nothin'.

Feel somethin'!
Walk coals. Tarry round the altar all sweaty
Screamin' and bukein' resilient demons
Sweat your hair back.
Have your Grandma come
'Tend you in the house of God
Pullin' out sins your nine-year old self can't be.
Open your mouth. Shout. Shout in tongues
And run the aisle shakin' your fist at God.

Feel something!
Beat upon your chest
Get rhythms goin'. Call the ladies from the pews
　　To dance
Have them hike their skirts and fall
Layin' lap-rags over thighs
So the men can't see
Paradise locked-up.
Beg 'um to teach you to dance. . .

Beg 'um to teach you to fall. . .
Beg 'um to teach you the secret
Of un-lockin' doors.

ABOUT ETERNITY

It's about how you feel about eternity:
Waking each morning
The dishwasher on the dry cycle
The clothes separated light from dark
And the peroxide
On the spots on the white panties
    With the bleach.
Today, there is no soy milk
The grand's don't like the no-name frosted-oats.
You make toast.
Mr. James cut the grass last week
And hasn't come back for his check
It needs cutting again. It rained the whole day.
Somehow you will have to pull out your work,
    Pleadings
And petitions before commissioners and magistrates
They will repeat the same old language
Over and over again and again in concentric circles
Having no position, making no sense.

You worry if you should go thrift store shopping
Your mama did for therapy.
Yesterday they took your sister
    To the emergency room
Ruling out stroke and heart attack
Never saying what they were ruling in.

You're scared of just about everything -
Growing older
Being immature growing older
Losing folk; some who stay around
That you'd rather go.

You worry
There's not much to cook tonight for the grand kids
You worry
If you'll remember Little D's eczema medicine
You forgot the suntan lotion
But stayed six hours on the beach anyway
You wonder if the sea gulls
Will eat the rest of your Fritos
They are fattening and you have brought a large bag
They eat some
All converging together
You wonder if they are too salty
You wonder if you strip to your blue Pieces' panties –
If the people at the beach
Will know that you are in your underwear.

The children swim long, hard hours
You wonder if you ever were a child
You never felt like one.

You remember Elder Michaux's Devil
And the demonic forces now
That float around the world
Your world,
Leaving him, pale, emasculated, and powerless.

You wonder
Why you got to go into this wilderness alone
Why you got to fight powers and forces
Why love can't just be love
Without institutional knowledge
Of every ill you've ever known
        Knawing into it.

You think about God.
You remember the Islamic Lady in "Fahrenheit-911"
Crying out to Allah
And you think about Jesus
And you think about absolutes
        And if the present
Dispensation of time makes any sense
In light of what we were taught was to come. What?

Wasn't it always about fear?
Five year-old sitting in a solid oak sanctuary
Waiting for the sky to crack and the trumpet to sound
And one - to be taken - and the other - to be left (Grandma,
maybe?)
Growing old, I cried to God today
        Because I still don't have a clue.
Use to be all we did
Was in preparation for eternal life –
Shelter, a bit of clothes - enough -
Enough to walk into tabernacle and sanctuary - Ready!

Hasn't it always been about blood?
Not just on a wooden tree hoisted over creation
But blood and gore

And the immensity of mass inhuman denial
Of other men's humanity.

Wasn't it always about eternity?
Wasn't it always about Armageddon
And armies marching,
And Islamic demons chopping off your head
     If you didn't renounce Christ?
At least – that's what Deacon Williams said.
Wasn't it always about surviving the tribulation,
About being here after the rapture
And the only way to get to heaven, then,
Was that you had to die in the name of Christ
And not take the 'mark of the beast'?

Hasn't it always been about trying to raise our head
     Above this dread
And see some sovereign love saying
I am glad you're here for a while, child
Sit down by this sandy beach and let the sight
And sounds of the waves preach redemption.

Just for today
There's no one-world government
No illuminati
No invisible weapons of mass destruction
No frightening dooms day-sayers
And players seeding our need to see
Jesus full and fluffed
On ruff media presentation –
     105 minutes. . .
          With 33 seconds per prayer
               And 45 for the benediction.

Isn't it now just about us all getting back to faith
Some small infinitesimal witness
That there came a time, a place
And a man
Who had grace enough to live
Because HE was one with creation
      And wanted to be one with us.

Wasn't it always about bringing us to life
      Instead of death -
I mean "LAZARUS, COME FORTH!" -
Laughter and joy instead of renunciation
Redemption instead of damnation –
"THIS DAY YOU WILL BE WITH ME…
      IN PARADISE."
Wasn't it always about more abundant life
Leaving these contemplations on eternity
In the hands of the ONE
Who always had our best interests in hand
      And who is always then,
            Doing the best for us.

THE THINGS SHE HID

The things she hid
Between leaves of the old bible
Between prophet and pastors
She heard
Not a word of comfort.
She lived above synapse
Closing soulful songfest
While Bessie
    Danced
        Down
            Her demons.
The things she held in abeyance
Her trance barren - merely natural happenings
Hyped by boom box brothers
And sistahs with a lap-rag.
She hid behind her kindness
Till its vapors dispersed all love
Leaving nothing:
    Nothing hidden
        Nothing to hide
            Nothing to hide behind!

WHATEVER

Whatever have I learned?
Whatever did they mean?
Telling me half-truth and lies
So hideous they hampered all the hope
Of the little child.

Children fair well on love
But their souls fade wading in the mire of dire gods.
What did they show me?
What did they tell me?
Hell awaits, and there is a gated entrance
    To heaven
Where only those of the "one way" walk
Are welcomed in.

My sin was not rubbing flesh the wrong way
In the stolen hours
But doubt and fear
And weary wishing for a sign
This time more real
Than 'the mand of God'
Nodding from the pulpit
Knowing all, but giving nothing much
Such that a little child can hold
And fold into her heart.

Old, old people slap their thigh
And die off in record number
Noting nothing,
Leaving no note for following behind!
Kinda' dank in here ain't it
Kinda' wishing there was another way
Except the way of the grave
And raving dreams of eternity stalking by
　　　Without a witness.

MEN WHO FORM CIRCLES

Girls with fine straight hair
And fair light skin
Slain in the spirit could bring the men
From the mourners' bench
And empty the bishops and the deacon's chairs
They'd be right there. Lord, what a cinch.
Cause God was a workin' and they were'nt a lurkin
But helpin' them poor lost girls you see!

But me, my hair was kinky, short and nappy
And not a soul moved (not even my pappy)
To form a ring round the places I would shout
To protect my little footsies when I was falling out.
Before you scold me and tell me I ain't fair
I just was a-wishin' for fine straight hair
        And men who form circles.

BREAKIN' PRAISE

Praise breaks swellin' sanctuaries
Sanctified sistahs steppin' sounds
To Saturday juke-joint jitterbugs
Come boogyin' to Moses' Melodies
Masked in soul-felt symphonies
Tightly tuned to bar-strings of the slave ship.
Those hips in spirited highs
Hallow the scattin' cries of Grandma Tave
Croonin' orgasmic organ runs
As tongues aflame
Proclaim through stalwart sage and seasoned sire.
Wind reed me now to fire
Come call/response
Conspire to
Dowse
    Dese
        Demons
           Down
Redeem the song
Of one so lost and definately damned
For here I am – confessed,
    Obsessed,
        Possessed
By generational hand-dance.

INKLING

So you get the inkling that you know
About who God is and who God ain't
You try to put it in plain folk language
Like He being the beginning and the ending
And the first and the last
And them who cast their lot with Him
Will be saved.
But, then you ask, Saved?
    Saved?
You just wants to know, is it a from what,
     Or a for what?
        Or a to whom?
Seeing as by the time
You think you got the answer
Three score and ten be bout run its course
And, of course, you done yo dirt
Thinkin' of the folk you hurt
Averting yo eyes and surprised
When like a pouncing tiger they rise
And strike a death blow.

You know about death
And the stare in the eyes
Of those standing at the door
Waiting for Lazarus to rise
And the anxious cries
When nobody come forth
No grave clothes drop away
And don't nobody speak a word
Don't nobody say
"Loose that man and let him go."

So you know, that you know,
That you know, that you know, that you know,
That you know, *that you don't know* -
But, you do love
Because love hopes all things,
Even though sometimes
You don't feel no love for nothin'.

But, the word out on the street, say worship
The word down from Sinai, say worship
In the spirit, and in the truth -
And you know 'spirit'
Is more than Hezekiah Walker walkin' ya
And Kurt Franklin talkin' ya.
So you test the spirit to see if it's real
And you know you had it shine on you
Break you into a thousand tears
Then calm your fears
Speaking peace in yo windstorm
Making you face forward
Then go forward
Cause tomorrow be destiny
And the past as gone –
        As the last lover you played.

So you have stayed
Down in the sistah circle
Dancing
    Down
        Demons
Screaming for just joy
To play upon yo' heartstrings

Just faith
To magnify yo spirit
Just peace
To fill the tentacled places of consciousness
Just Jesus
To fill the doubting spaces
     Of yo soul!

SOMEDAY

Someday
I will understand what God is talking about
And it will not be in tongues
    Of fire or flame
I will not need to know Hebrew or Greek
But, He will speak in plain English
And he will say
Go. . . or. . . come. . . or stay. . . or sit still
. . .Or move over. . . or see
. . . Hear. . . reject. . . accept
. . . Not Now. . . wait. . . not that, but that. . .
. . . Pick up the pace...slow down. . .
. . . Stop that. . . get up and get out of there
. . . Leave him alone – he's a low down -brotha
. . . Leave him alone - he's a down-low brotha
. . . Leave him alone - he's a fool
. . . Stop drooling over spilt milk. . .
Put on some make up. . .
Stop crying. . .
Split. . .
Run. . .
I Said Run. . .
I SAID RUN. . . RUNNNNNNNNNN...

Someday,
I will understand what God meant by what God said
And it will not be some archaic music –
    Up above my head
But, right in ya face
Plain as grace

58

Amazing as the light from under the bushel of a God
Who has no darkness in him at all.
And when He calls. . . I will say, Yes, Lord.
And when He says go…I will say, Where, Lord.
And when He says do. . . I will say, What, Lord.
And when he says give. . . I will say, how much, Lord
And when he says receive. . . I will open up my hand
And believe
Even as I open up my heart.

Someday, when I talk to God
He will nod his benediction
And I will not mistake it for license to do as I please
But as attesting the blessing of pleasing Him
Of loving Him
And living inside of His will
Filled with the message of peace.
Cause in that day when all prophecies fail
And all tongues cease
And all the knowledges of man vanish away
God will say
Laugh and I will say HA, HA, HA, HA, Lord
Play - and I will ring around the rosie all day long,
    If need be
He will say sing - and I'll say, AMAZING GRACE
Shout - and I will TWIST AND SHOUT
    Like they did last summer
And he will say Leap for joy -
And I WILL LEAP FOR JOY
And he will say dance - didn't I say dance -
I SAID DANCEEEEEEEEEEEEEEE -
And I *will* dance

Into the sanctuary
　　Prancin'
　　　　Under the shadow
　　　　　Of His Wing!

THE STORM

Oh, save me God in the tumult, come
Oh shadow this pitiful boat I ride.

THE THINGS OF GOD

The grace of God is learned in the storm
The way of God upon the wave
The voice of God in thundering form
Commands the depth of His power to save.
Oh save me God in the tumult, come
Oh shadow this pitiful boat I ride
Weary I am from the miles I run
Oh steel me in the rising tide.
Oh precious Word who wants my joy
Oh Word that blessed me in the night
Who stands with me in the midst of the storm
You keep my candle burning bright.
Dear God who won't desert the child
Whose cries the waves would overwhelm
Who hears the smallest whimper still
You're still the master at the helm.
Come now O' God who rides the wave
And bid me walk upon the sea
Redeem me with Your power to save
     And speak Your peace that comforts me.

TRIVIAL THINGS

They were trivial things!
How inch by inch
I let my hair grow natural
Forming it into long locks
And how inch by inch
Lock by lock
Dreaded-ly…they all fell away.
And what a-mourning there was
For just hair
Something mine
Not borrowed
Or purloined
Or copied
My hair-line
My face
My eyes – brown and bedeviled
And big in unbelief.

How they fell
Along the left side of my jaw
Then on the right
Swept to a just-right angle.
How beautiful I was then
How beautiful I felt
But then they began to thin out
Like friends
Like my further understanding of God
That was needed –
But day by day seemed to get a little shakier
A little more shallow

A little more like I'd forgot
The oil in my lamp
Like maybe too I'd forgotten
The potion needed for dreaded hair
To grow and stay strong.
Things were falling away!
Trivial things
Things that before I could hide
Or make believe they weren't there
So folk wouldn't get the truth I knew
That something was awfully amiss
Like patches of hair graying at the temples:
Always a falling away
Always a coming out
Always more flesh revealed.

It *was* the trivial things you know.
Nobody had died– at least not yet
But there was this expectation of loss
        And loneliness
And the anticipation of the two – together
Seemed like just too, too much to bare
It was easier to stare at the walls
        Blinking.

But, God winked and said get up!
And I got up because I had to
And I got up because I needed to
But more the matter to me,
I got up because I wanted to.
Not for this or that
Or for them or the other

I wanted to get up for me.
And this is making all the difference
In tackling trivial things
That in fact. . . do matter.

GREAT AS HE IS TO ME I WONDER

Great as He is to me I wonder
For the killing fields of Cambodia
Of Hutu killing Tutsi. Flesh of the same flesh
Bone of the same bone
Or that lone feel of chard to clitoris
Bleeding away all pleasure that raises seed
Or following the lead of the people
    Of the lie
Crashing the burning sky over Hiroshima –
Towers where I once walked lonely
Stone blown to free-fall flight
At the plight of those choosing ground
    Over flame.

Great as God is to me I ask Him
Of such death and decay. And that gurgling
Way, way down in the pit of faith failing into fear
And the clear sighting of the tomb
And every venture from the womb aghast.

Great as He is I am one of loathing anger
At how easy it should have been for Him
To say "be gone, be gone you demons"
Darkening the flesh of those I suffer to come unto Me
Still plundering every pulpit, pulling out every spec
From the tortured innocent
Still waiting the loosing of the millstone
About their necks.

Great as God is to me I weary
In my heart and mind
Of why mankind just can't be kind
And not reek in the blood and dissipation
    Of ourselves:
My ten million to your one
My extravagance to your poverty
My atheism to your faith
My faith against your faith
My children against your children
My arrogance against your fear
My intelligence against your deprivation
My health to your sickness
My violence against your passivity
My machete to your arm,
My penis to your vagina
My fire to your germ warfare
My weapons of mass destruction
To your sticks and stone
My freedom to your slavery
My total selfishness to your cosmic grief
With no relief from the first till now
And why and how this mockery locks tight
Duplicitous reason.
What is this treason of which I speak?

Great as God is to me,
And Christ the very image of his person
Pleading "Father save them that would be saved
And let His righteous rise from the grave
Remind them: that those of shuddering fear
Must seek the way of redemption
And preach the certainty of His coming day
    Of justice.

THE DAYS OF ME AND GOD

1.

These are the days of me and God
Before winter comes
Before brown branches bare themselves
And luscious leaves
Layer themselves leisurely on grass
And the sun turns cold
And the icy winds compel a covering
For the slayer slinks around and beside.
Well, I've a need for a hiding place,
I've a need for a resting place
A nesting under Your wing
A secret place where I can sing
In that turn from here to there
From eternity in you to eternity with you
These are the days of me and God.

2.

These are the days of me and God
Days of my coming through
Days of my praying through
Days of my saying to Him
Of all the things delayed
By fear and petty arrogance
Like I had a preference for
Whose hands the blessing flowed
I need your blessings
Not of money or fame

But a name of certainty
Clearly delineated on papyrus and ink
Untouched by editorial review.

3.

The days of me and God
He above and over all doctrine,
Disseminations and homiletics
Bared down to truth.

4.

It's relative, you know, our truth
Relative and meted out
As we fight over who's sitting there listening.
I've been a long time listening
Flitting about on the hot-seat
Not able to move.

5.

This morning the same thing
Full of indecision
Full of the same people I look to
For validation
And they, having none to give – give nothing!

6.

Don't want to debate you anymore, my brother
Everyone with an opinion writes a book
A billion-billion ink-marks of pen on papyrus
Telling it like it was
Telling it like it is
And me just waiting for a yes or no from You
To bring me peace.

7.

They say You're not a personal savior
But a corporate one.
Yet at 2AM when I am crying to You
At 2AM when so much has died –
     My youth, my dreams
My attempts to make things better that fail miserably
Those times I strayed so far from You.
Well, at 2AM, I need You, up close and personal
Involved like You are mine and mine alone.

8.

Did I tell You, Jesus?
The Catholics believe in you
Saying make our petitions to Mary and the saints;
The Protestants say, no, not Mary
But marriage and the family;
The Southern Baptist house the Klan;
The Pentecostals say tithes and offering
With Pentecostal bishops bare precious babies

While wearing prison chains in the pulpit.
Yesterday, the elder who seemed
    To need
        To make sure
I knew she was an elder
Told me her church was open to all beliefs
That everyone's point of view is acceptable.
And I kept thinking of
"No man comes unto the Father –
Except by me; there's no other way under heaven whereby
Men shall be saved."

9.

Most times I seek You, Jesus, through the eyes of depression
A heart of anxiety
Filled with angst
And ambivalence,
Knowing in the Spirit that you encompass all:
All that is around me
All that is about me
All that is beyond me.
And even though sometimes I rise from my mat
Of inability to focus
Inability to make decisions
Inability to 'feel' much of anything
Life so leaden down
So much fear that absent my joy, You will reject me
That in the abundance of my fear itself
You will judge me and find me wanting.

10.

And I have always been wanting
    To raise the levels of fluid
And electrical reaction in my brain
To worship you
In our place
That secret place under the shadow
That eternal resource
So my discourse with you in this life
Won't be so bland.

11.

These are the days of me and God
Days before night falls
And my fall into eternal waters
Living waters where I no longer thirst
Days of my looking up
Days of my reaching up
High above that third heaven
Into mysteries not to be seen
Into words not to be heard
Until I see You
And can be with You. . .
These are the days of me and God.

HEM SONG

You wonder when the pain will let up off your brain
When rain will wash nightmare into dreams
And you can stop screaming 'Lord, Lord, Lord,
What shall I do?
What will become of me?
In a sea of many witnesses I have stood tall
And all around they call me
Queen from the Dark Continent,
Warrior Women - wonder -
Well she rose anyway.
Wickedness was about
But she shouted down the nay-sayers
Shouted out her passion
And fashioned herself into herself.
She didn't know God could leave
She didn't think God would leave
And her grieving at his absence is absolute.
She became so small – a minute remnant of what was
    She crawled
Into the crack of the universe
And rehearsed her insanity
Pill and shrill dogma could not save her
She knew the end was near
She could hear the cataract billowing down the falls
Cascading over the jagged edge of rock
And she had cut her foot and bled all along the path
And no one brought a potion
No one offered a salve or balm.
She calmed herself by rocking to and fro
And knowing salvation was a singular leap

From deep sorrow
    To attest your right to love and hope.
If tomorrow will shine at all
She will have to sing her own song
She will have to bring her own joy with her
She will have to hope that God still loses virtue
    At the touch
        Of the Hem
           Of His garment.

FREE FLOATING

I have to find that place in me where God dwells.
That place, where, even in your rejection
I am still whole
I am still intensely
And intently alive.
I have thrived on a dream that was no dream
For a while silencing the little girls' screams
I believed in fairy dust
And witches dissipated in baptismal waters.
I have lingered long on this ledge
Pledging my life to myself and not another
And it's a lone formidable knowing
That there be no other way to be.
Not now,
Not in the twilight twirling its way about filament
And filtering through passions
Not now, not while, even in hot arms
Nothing's charmed or chimed about love forever after.
If I just have today. If I just have this moment
This millisecond
Of me not second guessing games people play
Or thinking that they slay dragons.
The walk with me.

I have to find that place in me where God communes
In tune with cosmic reality
I see things as they are
Not in some starry eyed wish
Or dish of pistachio poison and petrified anguish
And the thought of never-absence.

You will go, and on your journey you will find some other
voice.
That choice, made long before I cried for you
When all others walked way.
If I had my say, I turn back yesterday,
And we would be as we were:
    Children, needing each other
        Playing in each other's hair
           Saying silly things
And wishing the angels would wing us forward.
They did not,
They would not
For they mourned their own lost innocence
And ours was so, so lost
And the cost to will it back prohibitive.

I have to find that place,
Where absent all else, God reigns, and I gain
Some sense of something beyond
    And above holocaust.
It is not lost that I do not weep alone
It is not lost that others bare in them the same
    Tamed horror and fear
Of oblivion.
Well oblivion's not so bad
When the hurt is deep and sharp
And again, like all the other days, and weeks
    And times
You find yourself wondering, and wanting reason.

They tell me to write a poem of Joy.
   Well, show me joy.
They tell me to write of what is beautiful.
    Well show me beauty.
They tell me that in the midst of malignant legacy,
I must on this folded papyrus
Decline to cuss
And swear
And dare the gods that ravished me.
I stand with mouth agape
At the times I've fought this same old demon
And it rises defiant.

I have to find that place in me,
    Where, over and above it all
God calls me to something more than what I feel.
God, let heaven be real, and if not
Then let me fly away from this test without a prize:
It all seems such a waste of oxygen and care.

Beware the dark days I'm coming too
Beware the dark moments spent on the beach
Beside a beckoning tide
Beware the ides of March
And the somber days of hot August heat
And the neat little packages I save for rage
Beware, that coming or going,
No one knows the day or the hour of
For I've showered all the kisses I can on the dragon
    And he is not a prince
       And does not give way
         To princely things.

THIS

This!
Just this Just This JUST THIS
This way
Just this way...This Way...THIS WAY.
Just this way
Meandering on and on this way
To the end
This way to the end?
This way every day ending just this way
Night and day
Over and over
In and out
Night and day in and out
This feeling
Feeling this way
This way... This feeling ... No feeling.
Noisome tune crooning in a major key always
Over again always
Fat rat nesting in your chest
Heaving, breathing, leaving droppings
In brain slaughtered synapse
Nor-epinephrine carving crevices
Opening the tombs of my dead
Un-silent in my silence
Arguing, crying
Pursuing, protesting
They have counseled it
They have medicated it
They have consulted the oracle
Blowing blue/black smoke:

Totems still standing
   Demons still fanning
      The flame of this sadness.

DEPRESSION – DOWN ON MY KNEES

I been down on my knees
At 2Am
Telling God if He don't take this cup
I would drink it and be damned
And damn fool that I am
Here I am still alive
Snot runnin' from my nose
Sheet crumpled around me
Curly-cue in utero
Passing the windows
    So the demons
Won't come through the pane
And the pain leap from me
Or me leap from it
Bowels bused like Judas on the ground
At Gethsemane.

I been shunnin' shot guns
And showing up at social sites
Full of vodka and Tylenol PM.
I hate knives. I Hate love songs.
Most of all I hate holding knives
While I'm listening to love songs
Played in a minor key
Or see children prancing on the playground
Down by the waterfront across from the theater
Right by my church
In Washington, D. C.
Where I been down on my knees at 2AM
Telling God it ain't Him I be hatin' on

But just come and get me
And let me be sane
Or let me die screamin' Amen
Thank ya Jesus, and please
Please don't tell the grandkids I feel this way:
Way down here in the valley
Tryin' to pray
Tryin' to do everything
Tryin' to be everything
Scared to live
Scared to die
Scared to lie down
Scared to get up
Scared to jump
Scared I'll fall
Scared of the Pastor
Scared of the Deacon
Scared of Heaven, scared of Hell
Tryin' to be pretty
Scared I'm ugly
Scared I'm thin
Scared to lie
Scared to tell the truth
Scared to lie in your arms
Scared to ask the wizard
Scared to speak
Scared to be silent
Scared nobody's comin'
Scared everybody's comin'
And they comin' for me.
And they comin' to see me
Down on my knees at 2AM

Askin' God what fornicatin' is
Askin' God what fornicatin' ain't
Askin' God what blasphemy is
Askin' God why
Askin' for angels
Rebukin' Satan
Knowin' He's no red faced brotha
With a pointy-tail. . .
But, let your well run dry of serotonin
Let nor-ephrenephrin cake up around synapse
And we'll see who snaps during tarrying service
Sputin' epithets,
Speakin' in tongues
Bingin' on spit and tears and fears
Of 2AM mornings down on my knees.

And please, please
Isn't that the last sin I need to confess
Isn't that the last blessing I need to blow away
To pay the debt I owe creation
Isn't that the last time I need decline salvation
    And choose hell.
Hell, I been here before
Babies dying in Sudan
Two thousand in Haiti over and little water and wind
160,000 in Sri Lanka
 And the world *is* destroyed by water again.

I mean. . .
What's a little sin between friends?
What's a little frottage here and there?
And where have you been God/friend
Where were you when the lights went out?
Where you when I laid me down to sleep
And the weeping started
Where were you when I carted my behind
    Through the streets
And had to live,
Had to live. . .
Had to live. . . cause dyin' was an illegal legacy.
And that's all I could see written on my tombstone
Another one hits the dust
Another one busted down to size
And I could see JJ eyes
And I could hear Draea's music
And I could see Big D tellin' me,
"Ma, SOMETIMES GOD GOT TO BREAK US
    TO MAKE US". . .
And I could see Damo at Shiloh
And I could see India standing like a stone princess
And I could see Cierra and her peroets
And I could see Langston just bein' Langston
And I could hear Dia sayin "Hi Daughter"
And I just oughta get up from here
And I just gotta rise up from here
Pick up this room.
Wash my face!
What does food taste like?
What is water?
What is a hot bath in oatmeal soap?

Yes, damn it. . . I'm cryin'
Yes, damn it. . . I feel vulnerable
Yes, damn it. . . I need you to hold me
Yes, Damn it. . . it hurts
Yes, Damn it. . . you did it
Yes, Damn it...I did it to my self
Yes Damn it...and you,
And everything else than can be!

WOMAN!. . . What is that Book?
Woman. . . open that book
Woman. . . read that book
Woman. . . know that book
Woman...what is that passage
Woman...what does it say
Woman. . . hold it in your hand
Woman. . . hold it in your heart
Woman. . . what does it say
Woman. . . go ahead and weep
Tears ain't an indicia of cowardice
Woman. . . here it is
Woman. . . hear this
Pain don't last
It always go away
It reach its crescendo and then its diminuendo
Woman. . . sometimes the joy to come
Woman. . . sometimes the morning do break
And you gots to run on to see what the end gone be
It ain't about stupid
It ain't about crazy
It ain't about lazy
It ain't about worth

It's just you got to wake-up
It's just you got to get up
It's just you got to stand up
Woman. . . you got to stand strong
AND TAKE YOUR MEDICINE!
Woman you gots ta stand still
Woman you gots ta still stand. . .
  And seek your healing!

BLACK

I have been in Blackness so black
Black don't even know it be black
Night so heavy on me
Daylight had to trip by quiet
Less it rip un-ripened woe from the vine
And leave in kind its own mourning.
Seems to me, if you could see just a little Son-light
Just peer from under blankets of souless-ness
And bless the coming of day
Then you could play the dozens with tragedy
And have your say with holocaust
Boss it back with your knack for word and song.

Don't get me wrong
I've spoken to the leader of the band
And he be playing oldies but goodies
But blues be blowin'
From the think and broken reed of a sad alto sax.
What I lack is joy
Just enough to keep black at bay
And the braying hounds
    From sounding the judgment horn.
Gabriel be set to play blue-black notes
In rote repetition and staccato screams
Careen from the tem be drum
The tum-de-tum-tum of feet in Ghanaian frenzy.

My black be blacker than the closing of the eye
At the death-hour
Towering above me
Hovering over me
Walking with me
Toying with my joy-stick
Messin' with my praise.
I have day upon day of no contact with God
And as way leads on to way
I've come to wear black rather nicely
While the icy gorge below
Bellowing over the falls is calling every hour
The great falls tripping over jagged rock
With the ridge of hell just under the foam
Of the wave.

Save me God.
You who from the dark abyss
Kissed the deepest dark with Son and star
Who sparred with Leviathan and won.
Save me God.
You who declares what is and ain't
As the saints be dancin' down de demons
Down in the sistah circle
Shirt-tails whirling in Dervish-drunkenness
Black thighs absent the sign of the lying lover.

My black be blue-black
Berry-black-brazen
Brash-bigger-better,
Bitter-broken-bodacious,
Brooding-bold,

Burgeoning-bigot-boastful,
Beggar of a burly-black
And beein' neither cold or luke-warm
It be hotter than sun-stroke
Red-hot
Hotter than holocaust.

My black be blacker than my fist
To your cheek
A hissy-fit black
Where Jack Koerner and Little Miss Muffat
Sat and sprayed venom all over suffering.

Now I ain't one to pray wash me whiter then snow
Cause snow be cold and hearts be frozen easy
And there's the sleazy way soul tends to disappear
When even spectral light won't penetrate
And there ain't no hue to guide you over.
My black be blacker than midnight
Black so black
That I have a knack for walking
Shoulders bent cowering from sacred eye
When just above my head and in the sky
    A RAINBOW!

PSALMS IN THE KEY OF CHRIST

Of God I would write beautiful!
Of Him I would sing cantata!

CANTATA

Of God I would write beautiful
Of Him I would sing cantata
Pavarotti skills would fill the tune I hum to Him
With the sunrise.
Of God I would dance with feet boogying
For God I would run marathon
Be done with meager things
And on the wings of jubilant praise raise His banner
High over headline and byline
And my line of guilt
And pride over things I'd rather him not know
So I can go on with my doing.
But I am done with that and this
And seeking the worlds' friendship and losing His.
Count me as one whose yes is Yes, and YES, and YES!
As I bless the Lord with my best sacrifice.

I WILL PEN MY HOPE IN CHRIST IN PAPYRUS

I will pen my hope in Christ on papyrus
Mark it on misty morning mirrors
Adorn it with daybreak prayer
As my voice in spoken word proclaims it.
I will pen my hope in Christ on papyrus
And no alien gods defeat it or unseat it
As from the wellspring of my soul
    I set my feet to dancing.

I will whittle in wood this blessed assurance
And whisper it while walking by the way
I will dream my dreams of it,
And if, in momentary fear of death, I scream
I am redeemed by it
In His arms of sure salvation.

Every breath I breathe will delight in it
And on the narrow footpath as I walk
Scripting the leaves aside I will abide in it
And in the deep, deep hollow of all sorrow
I will declare the certain coming of the Lord
And retreat to his resting place.

I will chisel my hope in Christ in stone
Owning Him alone as Lord of light and Life
For little has he ask but that I know him
In the pardon of my sin.
Thus, I will pen my hope in Christ on the papyrus
Every movement of lip and limb will mimic it
Every question of my mind will answer to it

Every broken synapse will mend itself in praise to it
Every idol of offense will bend to it and find themselves
On fallow ground of utter rejection
Every purpose of my day will conform to it
    Anointed by it
        Chosen for it
            Rejoicing in it
I will sit in the circle of the saints and declare it
For my hope is in the Lord my God
And I will pen my hope in Christ
On the papyrus of my heart.

I TREMBLE FOR MY PEOPLE

 I tremble for my people who are no people!
They are no people because they refuse
To be Your people, My Christ.
Though housed in steepled sanctuaries
    And mega stadiums
With music blaring
And coffers burgeoning
They preach pathetic platitudes of wealth
And well-doing
All the while eschewing that faith
Fixed and sealed at Calvary for our salvation
Taught and preached on the dusty roads
By those who loved You
So that one day it would reach us
Along highways and byways
Lined with skyscrapers
And lights blaring through the night
Proclaiming no other name but your name.
They wanted us to know You
The way they knew You
Always expecting Your return with Your fiery flame
Ablaze in their hearts
Willing to die for You
But always rejoicing that they could live for You
And Your glory be the light of the world.

I tremble for my people who are no people
For they are no people
Because they refuse to be Your people, Jesus.
They like you well enough, they say,

Just You don't get in the way of their holding on
To stuff and fluff
And territory and titles
And positions
And manuscripts and manifestos,
And denominations and societies
And liturgies and programs,
And wafers and wine
And just enough time spent with you one day a week
So You don't ask them to change,
Surrender,
          And be free.
For they are "more afraid of freedom than slavery"
More afraid of the freedom
     And liberty in You, Abba Father,
Than rules and regulations,
And rituals of the law.

So, I tremble for my people
Who refuse to be your people.
Playing you against this or that deity
Giving them credence,
As if, there was some other sacrificial love
Demanding nothing
But a turning toward the lover that You are
And the husband of the bride that You came to be.

You didn't ask
For our babes tied to twigs a-flame
You didn't ask
That we perform gyrations and gesticulations
Or that we nation build here on this earth

To birth a legacy of mortar and stone.
You only ask that we own no other God but You
Name no other name but Yours, Jesus,
And receive no other spirit but Yours.

I tremble for my people who are no people:
They refuse to be Your people
And pray my tremblings cease
And we seek sweet release, in You.

SOMEWHERE...

in the "Not" of our understanding
Somewhere in those things
For which we wait and stand
Believing answers will come
And we'll be all the better for it
Those things mired in melancholy
Mangled by nightmare truth
Somewhere meandering in the netherlands
    Of consciousness
Places we are not privy to
Somewhere in the nowhere
Where all meaning must converge
Somewhere in the space of a blink
Or wink of eye
Where "I" stands lone
Listening to the soundless lullaby.
Somewhere in the no and the not
And not this ever more
Not a whisper
Not a wisp of wind
Not a breath
Not a sigh
Not a homing toward a heaven or a hell
Or the mouton meadows of the damned.

Somewhere in the watching of her hair turning gray
In the watching of her hair turning gray
Even adding a strip of blackening to it
And a bit of rouge
And a tuck, and clip, and snip

And still there are no answers to her questions
Like – Why DEATH? and Why ME?
And see here God, see here
The mere fact that I am mortal and can't understand
I still demand more personal intervention
And a laymen terms for Your take on oblivion.

Windstorms blow me.
Blow these dry bones back.
Blow back the sinews and the singing
Blow back my sight
Blow back the celestial
Breaking the barriers to my flight
Breaking the boundaries to my knowledge of God
Break the strongholds holding unbelief
Bare me up above the beyond
Bare me past the reasons for the unreasonable
Bare me past my passivity and angst
To the chance meeting of the stranger.

Who is the stranger?
Someone stronger than love
Someone stronger than death
Someone stronger than the vicissitudes of life
Stronger than the strife
And the knife-wound of pending tribulations
Stronger than my helplessness
Stronger than my hopelessness
And my peering into the gulf
Of the abyss.
My simple prayer if this:
Windstorm blow me

Somewhere where God is
　　To the mystery!
　　　　To the majestic!
　　　　　　To the eternal!

IF I DIDN'T HAVE YOU, LORD

If I didn't have you, Lord
I'd fall from the edge of the earth
No good word would know daylight
No small wonders cross my eye
I'd linger in solitude so deep
Angels would weep with me
If I didn't have you.

If I didn't have your strength, Lord
Brick and mortar and stone
Would own me
Doors would still be shut
No mooring hold my boat ashore.

If I didn't have you, Lord
What name would I call in mourning
What mercies at dusk
Forgive sin and misfortune
Whose footsteps carry mine
What manna cross my lips to nourish me?

If I didn't have you, Lord
Night would hold all terror
Barriers to Your spirit stand tall against me
Seas of weighted witnesses whisper doom
The tomb of my yesterdays pried open
Tomorrows laugh in my face.

Were it not for your grace, Lord
What dream elucidate my vision
What light illuminate my mission
What libation for my healing
What bread of life fulfill me
What pledge of love comfort me
Or heavenly dove o'er shadow me
If I didn't have you?

WELL, JESUS

Well, Jesus
How do I say to this people that You are real?
That in the still of an empty midnight
It's You I've called to fill my soul
That when the old, old dreams
    Came trippin' and talkin'
And mockin' and sayin" they would take this city
And folk offered little more than pity
I was sho' bukin' demons in Your name
And not ashamed of nothin'
Not anointed oils
Or testifyin'
Or cryin' round the altar all night long
Till my song come again.

See, I gots this music wellin'
But sometimes, Jesus...I just be smellin' mysef.
I be demandin' of You testin' and blessin'
While You be demandin' of me confessin'
And attestin' that my will be YOUR will
So's You can fill me up and out
And expand the things it's been hell understandin'.

You knows...I does what I can!
But Jesus there been days I been wrong . . .
    SO. . . WROOOOOONNNNNNG!
I mean what must a woman say
Of the arms that said I care
Then with my soul laid bare
    They stepped away

106

Or stepped back
    Or stepped aside
And it been only You to hide me
Under the shadow of Your wing.

Now You ask me to learn of You.
But You ain't that easy to know
It...Ain't...Been...All...That...Easy!
But, I still knows what's real
And I knows what I feel -
How I danced
In the circle of the saints
And spoke in an unknown tongue
Then run the aisles
Like Joshua circumambulating the wall
And how...In the thrall of that majesty
    You've parted many a sea
        For me to walk across
            On dry land.

And, I am still standin'
When folk thought I should fall
And I am still prayin'
When other folk be itchin' and twitchin'
And wonderin' how I made it over?
How I got over? How I got over?
My soul looks back and wonder.
See most times, JESUS,
I weren't tryin' to get over on no one
Just tryin' to live, Jesus
Tryin' to live!

Well, You give me a work to do
And when I said…Well, Maybe I could
You said…Chile…Just Do It!
And when I said, well, maybe I would
You said…whose stoppin' you
And I said well, "THEY"
And You said tell "THEY"
THAT - "I AM THAT I AM"
And I knows what I know
And they need to get wid My flow
So the spirit can move
And you catch the groove and grow
Into the woman
    I plan for you to be
        Into the woman
            I need for you to be.

Well, Suh Jesus,
I ain't askin' for no show of hands
And I ain't lookin' for crowd acceptance
Ain't watchin' exit polls
With a margin of error
Of plus or minus three percentage points.
I knows its your anointing
Pulled me
Kickin' and screamin' to my feet
Tellin' me defeat ain't no option for no child o' yours
Carryin' Your name
And rememberin' the stain of the old rugged Cross.

So...You the boss, Jesus
You *be* the boss
Though others ain't so sho' of You
They want You silenced
Want You banned from public school
(Well, we already did that, didn't we, and
look at the mess we're in).
They want You banned from public places
You...persona non-grata...not wanted here
Deleted from public record
Like history could exist without You
THEY WANT YOUR DEATH!
You, ridin' outta town on the back
Of eviscerated theology
WELL...I NEED YOU...UP CLOSE AND PERSONAL
Involved in every facet of who I am and what I am
I Mean RIGHT NOW!
    RIGHT HERE!
       IMMEDIATELY!
I won't go on without You.

Do, you hear me Jesus,
I won't go on without You.
 Can't go on without You
Because if in this life only,
    If in this life only
I have hope in You
I believe in You
I am one miserable son-of-a-slave
    Trying to be free
       But bound in chains.
So I'm naming every name, Jesus

Your Name, Jesus:
WONDERFUL,
COUNSELOR,
PRINCE OF PEACE,
THE MIGHTY GOD,
THE EVERLASTING FATHER
HE THAT WAS AND IS
    RISEN…
        JUSTIFIED…
            GLORIFIED!

Now, they can say You were the construct of Nicea.
They can play You off against Muhammed
    And Moses.
They can move You like so many chess pieces
From here
    To there
Or swear by Great Zeus You don't exist, Jesus.
They can even insist, there ain't some absolute reality,
But…they ain't me, Jesus,
They ain't me!

So, how can I tell the people that You are real?
I will kneel before You in confession
I will steal away with You in prayer
 I will go among the people
And proclaim the Gospel
    Of the love
        Of God
            In Christ Jesus
In Song…and Poetry.

SLOW DOWN SLOW

Slow down slow!
Get to know morning glory
Opening prayer to raise spirit from deep dark sleepin'
Weepin' in dreams for what was lost.
What do it cost to raise a song of morning
To clap your hands
And stand in the temple of your silence
Acknowledging majesty?
Just me and God talkin' and tellin' our secrets
'Cause we be friends
Talkin' as friends over coffee and croissant
And our want for joining.

Slow down slow!
Get to know mystery
Aching over past sins and shoulds
Don't do nothin' to please our God
At ease with folk just where they are
Just where He find them – torn
And worn
And havin' seen betta' days
And betta' ways.

Wake up soul!
Demons full of fright in the night-hour
Take flight at break of day
If you light that candle in your soul
And slow down slow
    To worship God!

SEVEN YEARS

Seven years I've travelled in this wilderness
Seven years of fear and unbelief
 Increasing anxiety and pain
As seventy times seven I've named the names
 I'm not forgiving or forgetting
While regretting and grieving and failing to thrive
In a land of yesterday and loss
Medicating change
Medicating the cost of not letting go
Attending the woe of all I hoped to be
But could not be
For want of real reason beyond life.

Seven years I have travelled in this wilderness
While death, the jester,
Painted clown faces on my truth
Dancing vacuous labyrinths around my joy.
There was no day absent angst or pain
And I could name every wronged wreath
Laid upon the tombs of my dead
The serpents head had not been crushed.

There was much to be recompensed, I knew;
Much in disrepair
And I'd declared war and swore revenge
For righteous reason for my anger
Entangled in ganglion in brain and synapse
That at last became much too much to bare
    With feet of clay.
There came a stripping away!

A purge
Of every maimed desire
Weighed in the balance and found wanting.
For all I wanted was Christ!
All I needed was Christ!
Not neatly packaged in rote rhetoric
And rigid ritual
But real and received in time of tempest and test.
The best of His person
Splashed upon the doorpost of my heart
His perfect will that all my wilderness wandering would cease
As I walk into His land of peace
And promise.

LAST NIGHT I KNEW YOU EXISTED

"Last night I knew you existed" as no other
Knew in spirit and mind and soul
That that other voice was not my own
But yours, confirming and informing,
"I love you my daughter," you said,
"I am coming for you,"
 My beloved bride, you insisted.
And though my faith was no faith really
You took what was there
       And decided it was seed enough
To birth and grow strong faith
Rooted in redemption in you alone.

Last night the dreams that disturbed and perplexed
At best, stood back and bowed to your Godhood.
You, the lone and only reason for my sanity,
You came to me, and the tears I cried in solitude
I now cried in your arms
And the fears that belayed each waking hour
Succumbed and scattered at the sight of your sovereignty.

See, last night I knew that you existed
And persisting into day,
The path you laid through nightmare
Is there, leading me through morning madness
Through this rush to be someone and something,
In a world that will not know you
Because they don't want to know you.

But, I want to know you, Jesus,
Not just in the nighttime prayers my heart pleads
Nor in the daybreak songs
Shouting from radio roulette
As shadows disperse
And the curse of man
        Is nursed and rehearsed before me.
I want to know you, Jesus, in everything I do
And everywhere I go
And in every breath I take and word I speak
And every exhortation I give before the sons of men
In every blearing of the lines
        Between eternity and here
I want to know you
And glow with the joy of your spirit
And rejoice in the presence of your salvation
And rest in the comfort of your everlasting love!

HE ALWAYS COME

He always come.
He always hear. He always listen.
Sit here. Alone. In the quiet of an empty room
Empty your mind.
Empty your heart.
Empty your soul.
Empty self of all the old, old things hanging
And banging and haranging.
Tell him the truth.
He won't bend. He won't break.
Tell him things:
I am lonely.
I hurt.
I am lost.
I can't go on.
 I am afraid.
I've failed:
Trying to bow down, but my heart ache
Trying to get up, by my soul ache
Trying to be strong, but feeling weak
Trying to stop the destruction
Trying to run on
Trying to be on target. Trying…not to *be* a target.
To cover all the bases…all the gaps
And spaces and places I have left behind all tattered
And battered and torn into pieces I can't repair.
Trying not to despair.
Trying not to mourn yesterday
But be glad for today and unafraid of tomorrow.
Trying to put all this sorrow aside

And not hide behind lies, garbage and acting crude
Trying not to be rude
Or cruel to those who have decided
Down is better than up
Those who abruptly choose death over life
When I choose life.
I choose life.

I am trying to live,
To stand up, Jesus
Trying to do all I can to walk like you
Trying to open my mouth
To say the things you said
To believe the things you said.
Trying to have faith
To pick up my cross
And not toss it aside disgusted
Because it means dying,
Dying, Jesus. Dying to so, so much stuff
    And fluff
Because it means dying to self.
So I am crying out to you, Jesus.
So sit here. With me.
And see in the quiet of your heart
If God don't part the waters
And bid you onto dry land,
Commanding your understanding
Demanding your attention
Standing right in the muck and the mire…waiting!
Waiting to give you the desire of your heart
Waiting in the quiet of your room
In the silence of the dark

Waiting for the bending of your knee
Waiting to free you
Waiting to see you conquer
    ALL FEAR!

JUST ME AND JESUS

Sometimes, it's just me and Jesus
Sometimes when the grands don't come
And friends don't call
And even if they did
There are places where I've bled
They can't see or even slap a Band-Aid on.
And it's just Jesus
Taking me by the hand
And making me stand up
Taking me by the feet
And making me stand still long enough
To know his will through the loneliness
    To experience his mercy
Through the only-ness of His Spirit
Speaking benedictions of grace
So I can run this race…In Victory!

OUT

Out from the birthing hour
Came this sorrow
And out from this sorrow in the world
A deep, deep weariness in me
Looking back at yesterday's sins
Paying over again and again for things not owed.
Out from beat down numbing pain
Claiming and proclaiming darkness
Black as the shroud for the dead
Out from it all
    I lift my head and sing

And out from my song
 Marvelous melodies flow
Hearty black notes upon staff
Careen from grace gathered
In the secret place of the Most High
Where I've come alone
To worship.

And out from that worship
A voice
Lifted up
Hands suspended in the air
Declare the certainty of the everlasting
My feet beat in exaltations
And in the circle of the people
From the wellspring of my heart
From the center of my spirit
I bow my head in prayer.

And out from that prayer
A thought
A talk. God in call/response
Assuring and blurring the chasm
Between heaven and earth.
Spirit doves high
Above the pinnacle of this temple
Lead a wayfarers wandering
To the seat of praise.

And out from that praise
Creation merits adoration
This mystery beyond history
This deity incomprehensible
This love exceeding love
Capable of nothing but credulous truth.

And from that truth He came
Stronger than the midnight blackness of my soul
Brighter than the sunlight golden of my joy
Out from it all I name
        No other name...but Jesus.

WHO AM I THAT YOU SHOULD LOVE ME

Who am I that you should love me?
Son of God, creator He

Came alone to save and shield me
Break my bonds and set me free.

I was bound by Satan's shackles
Bloodied by his darts of war

Little did I know the carnage
Was predicted long before.

You had warned me of the battle
Take the sword and shield, you said

I had sought some erstwhile helmet
For the covering for my head.

Till you pulled me from the warfare
Bolstered up my wearied soul

Taught me to prepare for standing
As they did in days of old.

With the word of life digested
Songs of praise upon my heart

Should the warfare stay before me
Hear my cry, "How Great Thou Art".

You the patient Master, Jesus
You the faithful word of God

Hear the poem I raise before you
Gifting from a battered bard.

That you love me, that you bless me
How can self contain my praise

See my pen has long been emptied
Writing of your wondrous ways.

FOR THOSE OF YOU WHO KNOW A WORD OF PRAYER

For those of you who know a word of prayer
For those of you who know me
I never said this life was easy
I never said this *way* was easy
That you wouldn't hurt
That you wouldn't need soul to soul resuscitation
That you wouldn't be in pain because of the aim
    Of the enemy.

For those of you who know a word of prayer
I never said you wouldn't weep
That you wouldn't get angry (I did)
Because other's have hurt you, or abandoned you
Or that you, being flesh, wouldn't hurt others
    (You know you do).
I never said you wouldn't know residual loss:
That abuse you suffered years ago
That before you know it is back…in memory…in flashback.

I never said those storms wouldn't come
Storms chile
Not little drizzles, not little droplets of rain
But storms. Raging through broken synapse
Tearing up your soul-space
Hurricane, earthquake, tsunami
Storms chile, into your life to test your faith
To prepare you
To rescue you from the thought
That things gonna be done your way
Storms chile, to teach you to stand.

For those of you who know a word of prayer
I never said this wasn't warfare
That it wouldn't feel like nuclear holocaust
That you'd never battle the one
Who steals, kills and destroys. I said put on my whole armor
Take my cross upon your back
Take my yoke around your neck. It's easy!
Take up my burden…it's light!

For those of you who know a word of prayer
I never said you wouldn't sin
But that if you did sin
I was your advocate with the Father
I'm your counselor (fire the other one).
I never said you wouldn't fear death
I said that if you didn't believe in my promise
Of eternal life in this life – that you would be miserable.
Most miserable!

For those of you who know a word of prayer
What I said was
Weeping was only for a night
I'm not going to run away from you
I'm not going to forsake you for someone else
My grace is so sufficient that on the closing of your eyes
That day, you will be with me in paradise
What I said was…you are mine
What I said was…I love you.

I TELL HIM

I tell Him, Jesus, If You walk outta here...
Then, I'm outta here!
If the Cross and Calvary don't mean nothin'
Let's stop the show right here, right now!
 I Tell Him...If there is no crown in glory
And this never-ending story stops
Right here in this place
On these dusty streets, between these dusty sheets
And the cleats of my feet just be diggin' down dirt
But ain't about walkin' in The Way
Or believing what He say.
And it be just 'easy listenin' Radio
Playing the same old tunes
Picking the same old wounds
Then... I got other places to go
And other folk to see.

I tell Him if He ain't real
And the Blood He spilled
Was just Scorsese and Demille on some Hollywood set
Directing the flood and the blood
And the saints through the fiery flames
And me. . . the name I been naming
Is just some feel good Sunday-Mornin' hoe down
With my feet and stoppin'
My hands a clappin'
My mouth a rappin'
With nothing more to show for it at the end
Than some gold statue on some bronze rock
And I's still rotten in the ground

126

And bound to this earth
Wid no sound of ole Gabriel
Playin that bold note
To call me home to Him…in him,
Then tell the boys wid the camera that's a wrap
And I'll be at the beach
Cause this…this be a breach contract
I's goin' home to watch Seinfeld.

And, I says to Him again
Friend
Jesus
If the prophets be lyin'
And the preachas be lyin'
And the matriarchs be lyin'
And the patriarchs be lyin'
And all this cryin' on my bed at night
Speakin' to Him
Callin' to Him
        Seekin' Him
Asking for Him
Waiting for Him to come
Cause He said He would come
But He ain't comin no how, no ways
Then stop bothering me, does Ya hear
And stop pestering me
Be silent!

I tell Him if Him neva' leavin'…
And neva' forsakin'
Is just poetic license
Written in some four-thousand year old musty book
By some musty dudes
With some musty beards
With a penchant for big words like
Crucifixion and Resurrection, and Pentecost and Salvation
And Forgiveness, and Sanctification
And peace on earth, and heaven, and hell and eternity
And Jehovah Jireh, and Jehovah Shalom,
And Jehovah This and Jehovah That,
And God in Christ Jesus,
I tell Him if it all be just some "King James" construct
With Shakespeare at the Dell
To please us, and tease us, and appease us…
Then I might as well read the comics
And Superman be the only hero I needs to know.

But, you see because I know Him
As The Man of sorrow
Knowing my tomorrows before I get there
Paving my footpaths before I walked them
Hearing my words before I utter them
Knowing I would rise up through the doubt and the fear
And the tear stained pillows
And the wilderness wanderings
And the testings and confessings
And ultimately the blessings
I'll serve Him.

And because he walked on the waters
And calmed the waters in my life
And sat there, gently sat there holding my hand
And walking on sand places
With only the traces of one footstep,
His footstep
Mine forever anchored
Mine forever hidden in his
Then, I thank Him.
And because on the inside where it counts
Under the covers where it hurts
In the shadow where my own darkness dwells
In the places of angst
In the turmoil
In the depression
In awakenings joy
In the harbingers of hope
In the secret place of the most high
In the Spirit!!
    He abides with me
        And I with Him…
            And, I surrender!

UNMOLESTED

"To be left unmolested by satan is no evidence of blessing"
C. H. Spurgeon

Like let me say dis to ya, baby
Let me say dis from de start. Dis life Be hard
Dis life be hard like de rock O' no apology.
And when ya finally accepts it
When ya finally settles inside of it
And lets its it settles inside of ya
And ya ain't hiding behind things to escape it
Like de kings of dis world
Or de apron strings of o' some so, so floozy
Prayin' unholy benediction
And directin 'n predictin' protection from dem also, so-so lost
Dat dey ain't counted de cost neither—
    No way—
        No how.

Let's me just points dis out honey. Dis life be hard
Dis life be hard like de tip of irons
Hardened in coals of fire.
And when ya finally gets the point of it
When ya finally stop smokin' a joint for it
Or thinkin' Hennessey can lift it
Lookin' for Sistah Shakra -- to anoint it
And Bro Hinn to amend it and send ya a book
Or a tape, or some oil from de olive tree in Jerusalem
Or a cloth draped over the Shroud of Turin
Sayin' change yo name now baby, you a prophet
Or follow me baby, I'm the apostle

And I demand yo tithes, offering, works,
And in return for $365 bucks-365 blessing will flow
Mashed down, pressed together and runnin' ova
"Can ya say amen? Allelujah!

Nah, Wait! WAIT! Lets me tells ya dis, chile
Lets me pulls ya aside jes for a while and tells ya
Of the miles I done walked all in my pride
Like I can do dis on my own
Like I could approach Christ throne
Someday…
Someday, when I gots a minute
Someday when I done finished my courtin' –
Finished my education
Finished raisin my chillin', writin' my book,
Finished bein' mad at dem dat done made me mad
And I's sadly come to dat time when I's a bit long in de tooth
Tryin' to fine a sure escape route from hell.

I tells ya, dis life be hard!
Dis life be hard as my heart, once frozen in sin
Till I gots sick of dat sin- my sin
So sick of my sin, so - so sin-sick
Till I had to pick up my eyes and looks to de hills
And find dat my help come from de Lawd
I had to open my eyes and realize: DIS BE WARFARE:
Satan ain't declared no line of demarcation
He all over de place tryin (cuze me)
He all over de place for real—stealin'
      And killin' and destroyin—
(Remember Middle Passage! Remember The Holocaust).
He all over de place in yo face.

133

Dis ain't no war game, you know- in de woods
Wid de blanks bullets and toy grenades
Where we parades outta here wid de fake blood
We gone wash off and have good meal.
Dis enemy wants to steal your life!
Dis holocaust
From de boss of dis world
    Will can cost you
        Your soul!

But there is the way of de cross
With the shield of faith and the helmet of salvation
    And your feet
Shod wid the gospel of peace
And the sweet release of the Holy Spirit into yo heart
Dat old, old story coming from de start of de world:
    No other Spirit but God
        No other God but de Word
            No other Word but Christ.

GETHSEMANE

In the garden where Christ paid
And laid upon the altar of God
Tears of blood thick with the weight of the people
Soiled with the sin of the people
Becoming their sin
Dying in their place
Down in the desert garden by Himself.

In the garden where He left
All to his Father's will, still in His passion
Feeling the nails driven spike by spike
Pure righteousness took up our wooden cross
That no one else could or would
He stood exposed and rejected and subjected to scorn
Down in the desert garden by Himself.

In the garden where Christ mourned
Morning stopped – the veil torn asunder
As Wonder blotted our transgression on a timbered tree
As He remember you and He remembered me
Down in the desert garden by Himself.

THESE DAYS

These days
Still the same twenty-four hours
Weeks divided into seven
Months into twelve
And all my well-meaning answers
Turn, position, change
And posit more of the same
While I keep trying to name that tune
Crooning in my head
Fed by arrogance and pride
Having lied to me all these days.
These days
Gray hairs on head and chin
And I'm not winning any marathons anymore
Any more than I did
Running about the sanctuary trying to please God.
Oddly, He just wanted me to sit down
And sit still
And feel the willing of his wonder in the universe
Where He painted the bluest sea
Just for me to see His glory pressing through.
These days
Laid out like the tracks of trains
Going nowhere and everywhere like eternity is
An all
    And a nothing
        And a less
            And a more
Circled outside of time
Told in midnight majesties.
These days
Hellish and torn
Adorned with God-light
At the sight of my soul in worship.

MANY TIMES

There are many times
When my skies are gray
And my way is long and hard
That the only place that I find to turn
Is to the face of God.

There are rails I've traveled
All alone with complicated task
But, I have sat in the arms of God,
What more could a traveler ask.

There is mountain, valley, pit and stream
And folk who will not share my dream
Of peace and worship for they say
Is there not less a committed way
But, see…I mean what I mean.

For when I raise my arms to God
And when I bend my knee
All that I am and all that I'll be
Beholds eternity.

Now, I have been to the house of pain
And I have been through the fire
But only in the house of prayer
Does faith conform desire.

And my desire is not of wealth
Or fame or fortune or greed
But, give me the standard of Jesus name
It is really all that I need.

There are days I have
When my skies are blue
And my way is fair and free
And the Love of Christ I gladly wear
His banner of Love
   Over me!

NIGHT INTO DAY

Night into day
The way of God unfolds upon our sorrow
And meaning writes itself upon the papyrus
    Set before us.
We tell and old, old story – old demons threatening
But they are vapor and hologram
For here I am still standing
Standing still in the waters of my tears.

Night into day
Fear fills synapse with secrets
Bound in heart and mind
I find my soul empties
My spirit sifts bare and stripped
And I lift my hands to the countenance of God
Sustaining me and not blaming me
But reclaiming me in the wellspring of his love.

Night into day
Somehow the morning breaks
And whispered in the song of new birth
A new refrain:
The voice of God calling me
The heart of God holding me
The promise of God enfolding me.

EBENEZER

Hitherto the Lord has brought us
Through the desert-lands and dust
Band of travelers longing homeward
Full of dull dreams and disgust.
We were worn from weary workings
Whips and shackles on our back
But the promise stood before us
Wondrous land that knew no lack.
So we left that night rejoicing
Hellions hunting every step
Yet a fiery cloud would tarry
Turn them, spurn them to their death.
See we're standing on *That* landmark
Hallowed one of our delight
He the cornerstone rejected
Raised in majesty and might.
Hitherto our God has brought us
To the promise of His son
Give Him glory, He is worthy
Christ Alone!
That stone!
That One!

TO THANK GOD

To thank God for life
To thank Him for the winds of change
And the chains now broken
And the words spoken in the sistah-circle
In the midst of the sanctuary
In the city of hope for all things good
Coming to those who love the Lord
And are called according to his purpose.

To thank God for test
Coming in from the whirlwind
Of past sins and shoulds and woulds
That you rather not recall, but all the while
Reminding you time and time again
That you cannot win
With the past in front of your face
Put it behind you as the grace of God renews you.

To thank God for spirit
Walking with you
Lifting you up
Sometimes reaching down in the muck
        And the mire
                And picking you up
When you haven't the will to stand
Taking your hand in the darkness
And walking you to the light
When night is heavy on you
When night threatens your destruction
When night threatens your very soul.

This thing about growing older
Is that there is something within
That makes you bolder
Makes you know the source of all hope
Makes you know the paths
You must not walk again
Makes you know the words
You must not speak again
Makes you know the friend
You have in Christ
Is the best of friends.   And in the end
You need to thank Him for just being God
Always there, always aware
That you need Him.

EPILOGUE

WORD

How word came to me - how it was handed me?
When my father in his passion and his pain
Planted himself in my mother
And there was a mixing and a mingling
Of love and hate
Of bone and sinew
Nerve endings and synapse
Synchronicity manifest in one bursting forth of his substance
A calling forth of another soul unwilling
And unknowing
And not much of a mind for death.

How it came to me?
Arms too wounded to wrap themselves in touch
A voice too muted to hum the loving lullaby
How it came to me in that silence
And how the serpent danced around that ground.

How it came to me – how it was handed me?
My grandmother Tave, and the stories she'd tell
Bout "Martha, didn't yo motha tell you not to go"
And the switches broken from birch trees
And the unrelenting hair she platted and pressed
And the dresses we wore – two days in a row then washed
And wore again.
And the truth's she'd tell four girl-children –
Gathered about her
How my daddy left, then died in a room
Where they found him three days later
And lay in a morgue
'till they buried him three-month later.

How it came to me - how it was handed me?
How it came to me, and it was mine to accept or reject
How it was all confusion - diversities of confusion
And incomprehensible enigma.
How it was between God and the gods
At odds with the stuff of time and totem
At odds with the stuff of control and choice
Judgment laid down
A cloistering in
And a cloistering out of things misunderstood and molded
Things ancient:
Carvings in bone and stone
And anthropomorphic mettalia - shriveled heads
And star-gazers
Mediums and sorcerers - witches in wonton gyrations
Gesticulations and circumambulations –
Humpings and bumpings
And vestal virgins feeding ferocious fires
Progeny sliced, slithered, and sacrificed
On the altar of gluttonous deity.

How it came to me - how it was handed me?
Not of Mecca or Medina
Or the sage of Sakya or Sanatana Dharma
Or walking the red road
Or Voodoo and Ifa, Santaria and Candoble
Or a Yaki way of knowledge and peyote plants,
Or Star beings and buffalo - Masonic rituals,
And new age crystals channeled by spirit guides
And Rastafari in pass life regressions
And transcendental meditations.

But, how in the deathly darkness
In the least of all cites - at the least of all times
One had come -
A voice calling through the wilderness
Confounding them with his Godhood
Cajoling them with his passion for them
Weeping for them in a lonely garden
Bleeding for them on a timbered crucifix
Endeavoring to lead those who would not be led.
And how I would not be led
For I was lost
    And I was everyman.

How it came to me - How it was handed me?
How it was mine –
A private matter between me and God
And the lovers I had laid
And made for what they could give -
Or for what I could take or break away from them.
How it came to me as pathos of the homeless in Dupont
As twenty-eight thousand to volcanic ash
As hair-sprays and smell-sprays
Warming the global atmosphere
As the genocide of abortions
The genocide of AIDS
The genocide of African Killing
    And maiming African
The deception of democracy
The deception of materialism and prosperity doctrines
The deception of love forever after
The reality of death.

As a thousand thunderings in this whirlwind,
As a million questions with null answers;
All this was handed me. There was no audience,
Neither hand clap nor pat on the back
Or a "speak sistah speak" in tactful linguistic propriety.
Nothing was incorporated or amalgamated
Or wrapped in laminated apostasy
It wasn't about dresses or tresses
Or whether the lauded laureate bestowed the laurel
Or the precha preyed a few words from the podium.

All this was mine…
Mine and the silence at East Potomac
Mine and the river bed
Mine the shroud for tongue
    Cleft to roof of mouth
It was mine and the rain
Mine and the pain I have felt
And the sins I have committed in secret
And the demons I alone have conjured
And the blues I cried for my own trepidations
And the malignity of my own imaginations.
All this was handed me,
And I bore it like a rugged cross.
All this was handed me
And I wore it like African nobility,
Carved it in tribal mask
Stored it in pretty dishes
Played with it – prodded it with my hand–
To make it stand
For you who would not stand,
For you were cold - and no longer dreamed of it
For you were old - and no longer esteemed it.

But, Oh, how it threatened its absence
And defied my silence
And came lisping,
And talking
And disputing
Caring little if it offended or pleased.
And Word said to me:
"See these things," and I Said "Yes, Lord!"
And IT said, "Well, write of these things,"
    And I Said, "Well, Yes Lord!"
And then IT said, "Now go out among MY people
    And speak of these things,"
And I said "YES...MY...LORD!"
And there...was the poem
And I...was the poet
And it was all good!
    And all the Glory...
        All of it!
            Belongs to God!

152

ABOUT THE AUTHOR

Billye Okera was born (Evette Billye Epps) in 1950 in Washington, D. C. and She has been writing poetry since the age of seventeen. For 15 years she was a founding member of the poetry group Collective Voices and performed with them throughout the DC Metropolitan and surrounding areas, and in London England at the Brixton Theater. In 2003 and 2004 Billye presented her one act plays "Stages and The Mourner's Bench. Her book *"The Mourner's Bench—And Other Stations of Weeping and Joy* received a nomination for best poetry chap book from the National Underground Spoken Word Poets (NUSPA)in Northern, Virginia. In 2001 Billye was chosen as one of five "POETS in Progress" by the Poet Laureate of Washington, D. C. Billye writes across a spectrum her own life dealings with sexual abuse, depression, but ultimately faith. This book is given as tribute to and solidarity with *ALL* who have done the questioning…the weeping…the walking…and the awakening to the wonderful realization that *it's **ALL** about Christ and Christ alone. Billye is the mother of three and grandmother of eight and resides in Ft. Washington, Maryland.*

www.ingramcontent.com/pod-product-compliance
Lightning Source LLC
Chambersburg PA
CBHW072143090426
42739CB00013B/3270